Stevenage

IN OLD PHOTOGRAPHS

The Cromwell Hotel (The Moat House), *c.* 1920. The middle part of the hotel was built in the mid-eighteenth century and was originally a farm. It remained a private house until the early twentieth century when it became the Central Commercial and Family Hotel. At this time it began to be known as the Cromwell Hotel as it was said that John Thurloe, secretary to Oliver Cromwell, lived there in the seventeenth century. There is, however, no evidence to prove this story.

Stevenage

IN OLD PHOTOGRAPHS

Compiled by MAGGIE APPLETON

Alan Sutton Publishing Limited
Phoenix Mill · Far Thrupp
Stroud · Gloucestershire

British Library Cataloguing
in Publication Data

Appleton, Maggie
  Stevenage in Old Photographs
  I. Title
  942.582

ISBN 0–7509–0241–8

Typeset in 9/10 Sabon.
Typesetting and origination by
Alan Sutton Publishing Limited.
Printed in Great Britain by
Redwood Books, Trowbridge.

First published 1993

Contents

	Foreword	6
	Introduction	7
1.	Old to New	9
2.	On the Move	37
3.	Fun and Games	57
4.	People and Personalities	81
5.	Just the Job	93
6.	Events	113
7.	At Your Service	129
8.	Schooldays	147

Foreword

Like many married couples in the 1950s, we lived with in-laws in a small flat in London. Our move to Stevenage in 1958 was primarily to obtain a house, and more importantly, a garden. How little did I realize during that first year to what extent my wife and I would become involved in the life of the New Town of Stevenage.

The pioneers of the New Town were individuals. They were different people from different backgrounds but were united in a common purpose. That purpose was to improve their way of life.

For me, I am proud to say, Stevenage has fulfilled and exceeded the hopes and aspirations of those early years. As a Councillor (for more years than I care to remember) I, together with many other councillors, have been involved first hand with many of the projects both past and present. The Council has always focused on the needs of the community and through community centres and support organizations it gradually nurtured what is now a strong and independent network.

The photographs in this book brought back so many good memories of my life in Stevenage as well as a glimpse into what it was like before the New Town was even imagined. I thoroughly enjoyed reading it and hope you will too.

Councillor Bob Clark
Mayor of Stevenage

Introduction

Stevenage in Old Photographs draws together just a fraction of the pictures that have been taken of the place and its people over the past one hundred years. Apart from a few outstanding examples which demanded to be included, most of the photographs have not been published before. The majority are from Stevenage Museum's collection which has been donated by the people of the town since the museum opened in 1954.

The photographs have been chosen to show the people of Stevenage going about their everyday business and celebrating special events in the town. They show too how the town has grown and developed since the Second World War, from a village of around 6,200 people to the first New Town, whose population is currently around 73,000.

The book is not a comprehensive history of the town; it relies on what photographers have in the past chosen to record and what is remaining of their endeavours. Thus, certain periods, places and events are better represented than others. In Stevenage, two early professional photographers were Harry Wilton, who worked from Albert Street around 1899, and John Middleton, who took over Wilton's business from around 1902 to 1917. The expansion of the postcard trade before the First World War created a particularly fruitful photograph archive, as more recently have the records of Stevenage Development Corporation (1946–80).

It is useful to remember when looking at photographs that they can be misleading. People often like to be portrayed in the best possible light, so off will come the work clothes and on with the Sunday Best. Similarly, worries and poverty may be hidden behind a dignified stance. Nevertheless, photographs remain a valuable historical record as well as a source of interest and amusement. It is hoped that this book will prove to be both.

Maggie Appleton
Assistant Curator
Stevenage Museum

SECTION ONE
Old to New

The Six Hills, *c.* 1918. The Six Hills are the burial mounds of wealthy Romans who lived in the Stevenage area around AD 100 to 150. The mounds probably contained pots of ashes but their contents were plundered hundreds of years ago.

St Nicholas' church, *c.* 1900. The tower of the church dates from around 1127 and its walls are five feet thick in places. In medieval times the church would have sheltered villagers from attack.

High Street and Middle Row. Middle Row, in the centre of the picture, began as market stalls in medieval times but slowly developed into permanent shops and dwellings.

High Street, *c.* 1910, showing its unusual width. In the eighteenth and the first half of the nineteenth century the road was busy with cattle and stage coaches on their way to and from London on the Great North Road.

High Street, *c.* 1900. Charles Dickens wrote of Stevenage in 1861 that, 'The village street was like most other village streets: wide for its height, silent for its size and drowsy in the dullest degree.'

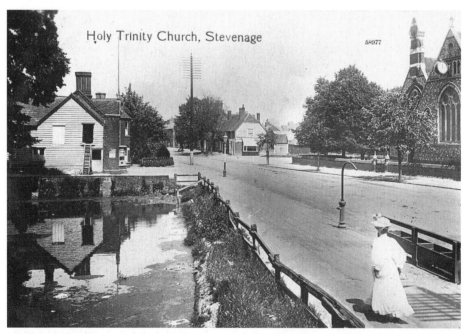

High Street Pond, *c.* 1900. Originally a stream ran along the west side of the High Street and drained into the High Street ponds which served as watering places for the cattle being driven through to London. The stream dried up some time between 1834 and 1851.

Albert Street, *c.* 1911, built between 1851 and 1858 and named after Queen Victoria's husband, Prince Albert. This was one of the first substantial movements of housing away from the High Street. Most of the street was rebuilt between 1962 and the late 1960s.

Julians Road, 1905. Julians Road is near the site of the old Julian's Farm, which was demolished around 1890.

Church Lane, *c.* 1895. Church Lane runs parallel with the High Street and because of its position was previously known as Back Lane. Some sources say that the name was changed around 1861 when Holy Trinity church opened but the Ordnance Survey map of 1898 still refers to it as Back Lane.

Tower House, Church Lane, *c.* 1970. The house was built by E.V. Methold in 1895.

Walkern Road, 1912–13.

Old cottages, London Road, 1906. The cottages were being taken down to make way for the building of Chequers Bridge Road. The one on the right belonged to the Dyke family, who built both the cottages.

Postcard of London Road sent from Stevenage in 1907. The photograph is looking south from the end of the High Street, with the opening to Gates Way on the right. This section of the Great North Road is now named Ditchmore Lane after a side turning.

The Bowling Green, Stevenage, *c.* 1910. Samuel Pepys describes playing bowls on the green in his diary in 1667. He was staying opposite the bowling green at the White Swan Inn (now The Grange), which was an élite hotel for carriages in the seventeenth and eighteenth centuries.

Green Street, *c.* 1900. The street got its name from the family who owned the big general store at the corner in the late nineteenth century.

Corey's Mill, *c.* 1870. The mill was built in the seventeenth century or possibly even earlier. It had four sails, a ladder, a tailpole and a timber roundhouse with a thatched roof.

Corey's Mill, *c.* 1895. The mill itself burned down in 1878 but the mound upon which it stood remains behind the public house.

Broadwater, *c.* 1900. There has been a village on the present site since Saxon times, when it was called 'Bradewater' after the brook which runs past – and used to flood at this point. A Saxon hut was excavated in Broadwater Crescent some years ago which suggested that either a settlement or an individual family lived here around AD 430. It must have been an important place at one time as it gave its name to the administrative district, or 'hundred', of Broadwater – which included Stevenage and several of the surrounding villages.

Rectory Lane, *c.* 1910. Rectory Lane leads to St Nicholas' church and many of the church's rectors have lived in the rectory here over the years.

Symonds Green Farm, *c.* 1895. Symonds Green probably took its name from William Symonds, who lived there around 1700. Previously it had been known as Woolwick Green, Hickmans Green and Rumbolds Green.

Townsend Close, High Street, *c.* 1930. In front of the house is Townsend Close Pond, the last of the town ponds to be filled in. Stevenage Motor Company moved into their new premises here in 1933.

The Town Hall on Orchard Road awaiting demolition in 1974. The Town Hall was built in 1871 and originally the police station was attached to it. In time the premises became inadequate for both functions, and a new station was built on Stanmore Road in 1916. With the coming of the New Town, work was scheduled to begin on a new Town Hall and Civic Buildings at the northern end of the town centre. As the town grew, however, it was decided that this space was needed for extra shopping provision and the new Town Hall has never materialized.

The Fox twins (see page 88) at work building the court house and police station in Stanmore Road, 1915. The *North Herts Mail* published this photograph in May 1915, noting the irony that two such regular visitors to the law courts should have a hand in building the new ones.

The police station and court house, before its demolition in the 1970s to make way for a new health centre.

Queue outside the Town Hall, 6 May 1946. The crowd were waiting to hear Lewis Silkin, the Minister for Town and Country Planning, who was in Stevenage to explain the New Town project to residents.

Outside the Town Hall, 6 May 1946. The Town Hall was so packed that Silkin's speech was relayed by loudspeakers to the crowds outside.

Lewis Silkin, with a crowd of journalists and residents, May 1946. The poster in the window in the background says 'Hands Off Our Homes' reflecting the fear that many Old Town homes would be swept away to make way for the New Town.

Inside the Town Hall meeting, 1946. The meeting was one of the longest and stormiest in Stevenage's history.

'Silkingrad', 22 December 1946. Clarence Elliott, who founded the Six Hills nursery, coined this name after Lewis Silkin's announcement that Stevenage was to be the site of Britain's first New Town. This had caused uproar, and on the night of 21 December 1946 Jack Franklin, with two of his friends (the sons of the local doctor), covered the Stevenage sign on the railway platform with their own version.

New Town sign, October 1952. The sign says, 'You are now entering the New Town of Stevenage.' It was on the old Baldock road, which entered Stevenage from the north.

Shopping centre at Burwell Road, off Shephall Way, *c.* 1963. The planners divided Stevenage into six neighbourhoods, each of which was to house 10,000 people and have its own facilities, such as shops, pubs, schools and churches, within easy walking distance.

Youth course at Aston House, 1958. Mr D. Rees, the Assistant Social Relations Officer, is discussing a model of the town centre with a group of young people.

Marymead housing, Shephall, c. 1954. By 1954, 862 homes and flats had been completed in the New Town, and a further 1,803 were under construction.

Housing in Elm Green, Chells, c. 1960. Building work began in Chells in 1958 and on Elm Green a year later. These houses were the first to be built to the American Radburn plan by which residents approached their front door by footpaths, confining traffic to rear access roads.

Radburn house fronts in Campshill, Chells, c. 1960. The system successfully separates pedestrians from the traffic but causes access problems for goods delivery and refuse people, and has confused many a visitor.

Town centre, *c.* 1958. This photograph was taken by J. Sainsbury plc, whose first shop in Stevenage was being built behind the crane in the background. The branch opened on 10 July 1958 and closed in 1968. The building was then bought by Boots and Woolworths, who took half each to enlarge their stores, which were on either side of it.

Queensway under construction, 1958. By Christmas of this year fifty-eight shops were trading in the town centre.

Queen Elizabeth II at the official opening of the New Town, 20 April 1959. In her three hours at Stevenage, the Queen unveiled a commemorative plaque on the Clock Tower and met officials, churchpeople and traders. She also visited factories, Bedwell Community Centre and homes in Shephall and Broadwater.

Queen Elizabeth's visit to Stevenage, 1959. In the background members of the Army are lined up where the bus station now stands.

Town Square and clock, *c.* 1965. The idea of a pedestrian shopping centre was discussed as early as 1946 in the draft Master Plan for the New Town. The idea was strongly debated and almost defeated, but a public meeting at the Old Town Hall in January 1954 voted overwhelmingly in favour of it. Building finally began in June 1956 of what was to be the first pedestrian shopping centre in Britain.

Town Square, *c.* 1960. The first shops began to open in 1958. Lavells confectioners and tobacco shop was the first, followed by the Co-op.

Clock Tower and Fine Fare, *c.* 1970.

Methodist church, *c.* 1905. The church opened in 1876 and the strong Methodist presence in Stevenage is no doubt partly due to the fact that John Wesley himself passed through the town on several occasions. There is a record of him preaching at the home of Mrs Anne Parker, a shopkeeper, on Friday 29 November 1782, when he was eighty-seven years old.

St Nicholas' church, *c.* 1920. This was the parish church from the twelfth century until 1960.

The church of St Andrew and St George under construction, December 1959. The church opened in 1960 and took on the role of parish church, as it was much more central than St Nicholas', which is at the north end of the town. St Andrew and St George remained the parish church until 1971, when the growth in population led to the six daughter churches in Stevenage becoming independent parishes. Including Aston village, Stevenage is now made up of eight parishes.

Junction of Hitchin Road and Julians Road, April 1973. At this time No. 1 Hitchin Road was being demolished so that Lytton Way could be built.

The south end of the High Street (west side), 1976. As the High Street is a conservation area it is protected from the radical changes which have been made elsewhere in the town. Some of the buildings behind the modern shops date from the fifteenth century.

SECTION TWO
On the Move

A horse and carriage making its way up the High Street, 1919. With the coming of the railway in 1850, and the end of the coaching era, this quiet scene was common in the High Street.

Outside the White Lion, c. 1920. The passengers in the car are Mrs O'Clee and her sons, who owned the butcher's business at No. 33 High Street.

Minna and Walter Cook in a Phoenix motor car, *c.* 1920. The car is parked in the drive at the back of The Poplars (No. 6 High Street) where the Cook family lived. The family was extremely musical: Minna taught the harp, Walter was a piano dealer and Benjamin Cook (their father) was described as a 'Professor of Music'. They also had two piano shops, one at No. 22 High Street and the other in Hitchin.

Halls Garage at No. 148 High Street, *c.* 1919.

Stevenage Motor Company, *c,* 1933. Outside are some of the first Morris trucks. The company began in premises at No. 15a High Street and moved to this site opposite Holy Trinity church in 1933 (see page 21).

Employees of Stevenage Motor Company, *c.* 1953. The group includes Jock Kindred, David Hemmings, Mr Mardlin, Mr C.S. Hodgson, Mr A. Chalkley and Jock Waldock.

Cars in the High Street, *c.* 1950. Middle Row can be seen in the distance, and in the foreground are Palmers the newsagents and the *Pictorial* newspaper offices.

Shelford and Crowe Limited, *c.* 1919. Shelford and Crowe was at No. 100 High Street and acted as both a garage and a motor cycle dealer.

Game's Garage, Nos 134–6, High Street, *c.* 1953.

Esso service station, Broadwater Crescent in 1959, the year in which it was built and opened.

Creaseys petrol station and car showroom at the junction of Shephall Way and Six Hills Way. The service station opened in the winter of 1962/3 opposite Stevenage Grammar School for Girls.

Traffic lights at the junction of Six Hills Way and the Great North Road, 20 June 1956. Eric Claxton, the Chief Engineer of Stevenage Development Corporation, was a great advocate of roundabouts as they allow a much smoother flow of traffic than lights. However, the Minister of Transport rejected the proposal for a roundabout at this junction because of the costs entailed. The lights were here from 1956 until 1967, when the engineers' wishes prevailed and a roundabout replaced them. As well as aiding the traffic flow the eventual roundabout reduced accidents at this junction by more than half.

Six Hills roundabout, *c.* 1970. The photograph was taken from the top of Southgate House.

Cycle track linking Martins Way and Almond Lane, *c.* 1970. There are twenty-six miles of cycleway in Stevenage. The cycleways are very much under-used today, but the engineers of the 1940s and 1950s could not have foreseen the car ownership explosion that was to take place from the 1960s.

Underpass at Six Hills Way being used by pedestrians and a moped, *c.* 1967. A fundamental philosophy behind the building of Stevenage New Town was that vehicles, cycles and pedestrians would be separated to increase road safety.

Cycle track at the junction of Six Hills Way and the Great North Road, *c.* 1953. The underpass goes beneath the railway line, and in the background are fields and trees where today there is the industrial area.

Steam train heading south towards London, after 1958. Beneath the railway line, pedestrians and cyclists use the underpass at Six Hills Way.

Cycle protest, *c.* 1954. The protesters are walking along the Great North Road in a demand for more cycleways and walkways in order to relieve congestion. The protest helped to prompt the building of the Bailey Bridge.

Stevenage Development Corportion promoting cycling in the town, 11 July 1967. On the far left is John Jones, and on the far right is Eric Claxton, the Chief Engineer. Third from the right is Alex Moulton, who designed the Moulton bicycles which the group are riding.

Flooding in Bedwell Crescent, 1968. The downpour on the afternoon of 3 June brought traffic to a halt and flooded homes and shops. The local newspapers reported that Stevenage was the worst hit area in north Hertfordshire.

Educational Supply Association delivery vans, *c.* 1960.

Railway station, Julians Road, *c.* 1910. The building of the Great Northern Railway began in 1847 and Stevenage railway station was opened three years later. The railway was a great feat of engineering as it was constructed without the aid of machinery. The building of the line through Stevenage caused a great deal of disruption to the town, not only when vast numbers of navvies camped nearby, but also because roads were severed by the railway line. The prosperity of the town was also hit as the road had brought travellers and traders through on their way between London and the north. Now people and goods could go straight through the town without having to stop.

Great Northern Railway station, Julians Road, *c.* 1920. Jess Usher is the porter standing in the doorway.

The old and new 'Flying Scotsman' trains at Stevenage railway station, 30 June 1938. The trains were at Stevenage to mark the fiftieth anniversary of the London to Edinburgh train. The engine on the left is the Stirling Locomotive No. 1 and on the right is the 4–6–2 No. 4498 *Sir Nigel Gresley*.

A steam train on the Great Northern Railway line through Stevenage, *c.* 1955.

Stevenage railway station in Julians Road, 21 July 1973. A Morris Minor and a Vauxhall Victor are among the cars parked outside. The station closed later that year.

The old Stevenage railway station platform, 1973.

Shirley Williams opening the new railway station in Lytton Way in September 1973. Shirley Williams became Labour MP for Hitchin in 1964, and following boundary changes was MP for Hertford and Stevenage from 1974 to 1979. She was later granted the Freedom of Stevenage. From left to right: Shirley Williams MP, Mr W.O. Reynolds (General Manager, British Rail Eastern Region), Councillor Hilda Lawrence, -?-, Councillor Munden (Chairman of Stevenage Urban District Council).

Bus station, Danestrete, 1962. On the left Swingate House is under construction.

Bus station and Town Square, *c.* 1981. In the background are ManuLife House, the Telephone Exchange, High Plash flats and Brent Court.

White Lion, *c.* 1973. Although Stevenage has changed dramatically over the years the Old Town still holds many visible clues to its coaching past. Notice how the modern door of the White Lion has been built inside the old coaching arch. Around 1800 at least twenty-one coaches a day passed through Stevenage, and many of them stopped here.

Fun and Games

Middle Row, c. 1900, The landlord before the First World War was Frederick Newberry and two of his regular customers were the Fox twins. They used to buy bloaters from Leggett's fish shop opposite and cook them on the pub fire. The Buckingham Palace ceased to be licensed at the end of 1919 and the sign of the Old Castle which can be seen in the background closed at the same time. The northern half of Middle Row escaped destruction in the 1807 fire due to a change in wind direction. On the right is the Buckingham Palace public house.

Stevenage Church Band of Hope, 20 July 1910. The group includes Mr Upton, Muriel Robinson, Mabel Upton, Miss Belgrave, Mr Hawkes, Stan Grainger (schoolteacher), Reverend Boothby, Alice Leggett, Fred Thody, Ernie Cole, Sid Smith (the postman), Cuthbert Tosher, Harold Cole, Bob Matthews, Charlie Ward, Clem de'Ath, Ernie Leggett, Alfred Pettengel, Les Upton, Bernard Davis, George Barker, Bill Steers, Guy Ellis, Fred Robinson, Harold Hughes and Ernie Breed.

ESA Brass Band, Bury Mead, 1898. Back row, left to right: Herb Wells, Fred Osborne (solo clarinet and conductor), Ted Harris, Bob Toll, Ted Farr (solo clarinet), Ted Cooper. Middle row, left to right: 'Murphy' Ellis, Fred Day, Chris Harris, Charlie Lowe, Jack Powdrill. Front row: Jimmy Osborne (son of Fred).

Stevenage Fair, 1907. The origins of this event go back to 5 June 1281, when Edward I granted Stevenage a charter for a weekly market and a three day fair each year.

Stevenage shop assistants' outing, 1920. On this occasion they were going to Bedford. The bus is parked outside Stevenage Club, which was at No. 31 High Street.

Stevenage Hospital Saturday Fund carnival float in Hitchin Road, *c.* 1924. Children from the Stevenage Wireless Orchestra are sitting on the float and Robert Field, a local builder and the owner of the lorry, is standing on the right hand side of the picture.

The Stevenage Players, 1927, putting on a performance of George Bernard Shaw's comedy *You Never Can Tell*. The play was performed on 20, 21 and 22 April 1927. Admission was 2d.

Baby show at the Roman Catholic rectory in Basils Road, 1929.

Women's Voluntary Service workers' outing, c. 1942. Their bus is parked outside the Emergency Hospital at No. 27 High Street. Second from the left: Mrs S.V. White; fourth from left: Miss D. Grosvenor; third from right: Mrs Griffith.

'Joyride' unveiling ceremony, the Town Square, 29 September 1958. From left to right: L.G Vincent (Chief Architect, Stevenage Development Corporation), the Hon. David Bowes Lyon (Lord Lieutenant of Hertfordshire), Franta Belsky (the sculptor).

The bar of the Two Diamonds public house, 1952. From left to right: J. Mead, B. Hemmings, H. Watson.

Stevenage Day Fête, 1959. The fête is being held on the King George V playing field at the south end of the High Street.

The Offley morris men in the town centre, July 1960.

The Astonia Cinema, 4 March 1969. The employees of the cinema are pictured on its closing night. The last two films shown were *The Thomas Crown Affair*, starring Steve McQueen, and *Submarine XI*. The management, afraid of attracting vandals, kept the actual closing date secret, even advertising future films as a cover.

Stevenage Scottish Society dinner at the BAC Social Club, Bragbury End, 28 January 1969. The haggis was piped in by Roger Hancock, junior member of Stevenage Pipe Band. Mr James Haddow addressed the haggis, Stuart Aitchison proposed the toast to Robert Burns, and the evening finished with country and mixed dancing.

'Figures with Doves'. A bronze sculpture by David Norris erected in the town centre pond in 1981.

Stevenage town centre pond, 1976. The pond was formed out of a spring named The Plash and was originally intended as a small natural feature. Instead it became the central attraction in the gardens that were developed in the early 1960s.

Stevenage Museum play scheme, 1984. The children were taking part in holiday activities about the Second World War.

Shooting party in Whomerley Wood, *c.* 1914. Standing up, from left to right: Mr Keen, Mr Cooper, Mr King, Mr W.F. Franklin, Mr Ansell, Mr J. Woods, Ben Moules, Mr Kefford, Mr Cooper, -?-, Mr D.A. Paine. Kneeling and sitting, left to right: -?-, -?-, Mr W. Croft, Herbert Matthews, Mr Keens, Mr G. Pallett, James Wright, Ben Clarke, Tass Pet. Lying down at the front: Harry James.

Stevenage Town Football Club, 1905. The club was called Stevenage Town until 1968, Stevenage Athletic from 1969 to 1976 and has been Stevenage Borough since 1977.

Stevenage Town Football Club, 1920/1. The team's strip meant that for many years the club was known as 'The Stripes'.

Stevenage New Town Rovers, 1904/5. The team is pictured in front of Southsea Road, which was part of a small new development of houses built in the 1890s. This led to the district around Fishers Green Road becoming known as the New Town. Back row, left to right: Ewart Kemp, Ernie Ellis, Ernie Tichfield, Chris Harris, -?-, Ted Harris, Alf Barker, Jack Jones, Harry Atkins. Middle row, left to right: Percy Simmons, -?-, -?-, Sammy Lane. Front row, left to right: Joe Austin, Billy Austin, Bert Leggett, Nelson Roberts, Albert Roberts.

Archery meeting at Shephalbury, 1905.

Stevenage Cricket Club first eleven, 1922. This is the oldest sports club in the town. A senior team was representing the town in the mid-1860s and early 1870s, and following a few lean years the club was reformed in 1877. The first full season at the new London Road ground was played in 1878.

Stevenage Red Cross Football Club, 1913/14. Back row, left to right: A. Aldridge, E. Day, F. Day, E. Boorman, H.J. Shelford, F. Chance, L.G. Upton (Secretary). Middle row, left to right: F.W. Munns, J.H. Matthews, E.J. Hunt, R.R. Kewarth, A.R. Upton, C.S. Chalkley, G. Barker. Front row, left to right: R.G. Cannon, H.A. Boorman, F.J. Day (Captain), R.G. Day, H.T. Day.

J. Tucker Peake riding a Vincent HRD
motorcycle in the 1932 Python Paley
Cup Trial at Telegraph Hill. The Vincent
HRD works in Stevenage was founded
in 1928, and the company became
famous for its high performance
motorbikes.

Educational Supply Association cricket team, *c.* 1940. The ESA was the town's main
employer before the New Town was built. It and G.W. Kings had their own sports
grounds, and played each other at several sports – the main ones being cricket and
football.

Tom Hampson winning the 800m final at the 1932 Los Angeles Olympics. He won the race in a world record beating time of 1 minute 48.8 seconds. Tom was a teacher at St Albans School at the time of the Games, and joined Stevenage Development Corporation in 1954 as Social Relations Officer.

Tom Hampson collecting his gold medal. Alexander Wilson and Philip Edwards, both of Canada, came second and third.

The ESA netball team, 1955. The woman throwing the ball is Joyce Atlee and standing round the net are Phyllis Abel, Pauline Hook and Miss Hunt.

De Havilland Football Club, 1958. In 1954 the Stevenage Inter-Works Sports and Social Organization was formed to promote sport and social activities between all the businesses in the town, old and new. Most of the large businesses and industries that moved to the New Town in the 1950s and 1960s were keen to join the Inter-Works organization. Playing or supporting one of the teams and joining in the group's other social activities helped the newcomers to feel at home.

The swimming pool under construction, 1961. Designed by officers of the Development Corporation, it was built to competition standards and with facilities for swimmers and spectators with disabilities.

The swimming pool, St George's Way in 1962, the year that it opened.

People and Personalities

Roebuck Inn, *c.* 1900. One of the most famous names associated with Stevenage is Dick Turpin, who is said to have stayed at the Roebuck on the way to visit his wife in Hertford. He was spotted at the inn by the local sheriff but escaped to York. Soon after he was captured, and in 1739 he was hanged.

'Grandma Clarke' at No. 16 Basils Road, 1913.

The Leggett family, Stevenage Hospital Saturday, 1907. On Hospital Saturday the people of Stevenage decorated floats and held a procession to raise money for the hospital. The Leggetts owned the fresh fish, fruit and vegetable shop at No. 90 High Street for fifty years. The Leggetts are, from left to right: Ernest, Ann (mother), Ivy, Uncle Alfred, Stanley, Cyril and William (father).

Double wedding of Ernest West and Rose Kirby from International Stores in Stevenage, and of Frederick Kirby (Rose's brother) and Rita Winters, 1910. The photograph was taken in the garden of No. 75 Letchmore Road. Back row, fourth from left: Phoebe Winters. Back row, fifth from left: John Winters. Front row, left to right: -?-, -?-, Frederick Kirby, Rita Kirby (née Winters), Frederick Kirby, Rose West (née Kirby), Ernest West, -?-, -?-.

International Stores at No. 122 High Street, 1912. Ernest West, the manager, is standing in the centre of the picture and Rose, his wife, who was a cashier at the store, is to his right. Ernest later opened his own shop, West's, at Nos 40–42 High Street (previously a wine and coffee shop).

Coffin of Henry Trigg, the Stevenage grocer, *c.* 1910. Trigg and two friends were on their way home one night when they saw a group of body snatchers in St Mary's churchyard. Stealing corpses to sell to surgeons and medical students was common practice in the eighteenth century. Worried that this could happen to him, Trigg stated in his will of 28 September 1724 that his body should be placed on the rafters of the barn at the back of his house in the High Street. His wishes were obeyed, although sometime in the 1800s the bones were transferred to a new coffin as the original one was perishing. The house and shop later became the Old Castle Inn and then the National Westminster Bank, where the now empty coffin can still be seen. It is thought that the bones were taken away as souvenirs by Commonwealth soldiers billeted in Stevenage in the First World War.

Kit Nash (left) with her family in Harmer Green, *c.* 1900. It is said that Albert Fox lived with Kit Nash in Harmer Green for a time. What is certain is that Kit Nash and the Fox twins were the best known local poachers of their time.

The Fox twins with their father, *c.* 1865. Henry Fox was a farmer and a lay preacher at the Ebenezer Baptist chapel in Albert Street. The twins were named Ebenezer Albert and Albert Ebenezer after the chapel.

Albert Fox, *c.* 1910.

Ebenezer Fox, *c.* 1910. The Fox twins are recorded as having over 200 convictions between them, despite using their likeness to continually outwit the law – by providing alibis for each other.

Outside the Red Lion public house in Woolmer Green. It is said that the two men first from the left and third from the left are the Fox twins. If they are, the photograph must have been taken around 1890. The Fox twins were known to drink at the Red Lion and these men are certainly very alike, but they appear to be fairly tall whereas Albert and Ebenezer were of below average height. Any ideas on their identity would be welcome at the Museum.

The Shepherd family at Shepherd's Yard, *c.* 1900. The Shepherd family business was founded in 1870 in Back Lane (now called Church Lane) by William Shepherd, the blacksmith. William taught his three sons his trade: William (junior) became a blacksmith, Joe a wheelwright, and James a painter and signwriter. Together the family made most of the milk carts in Stevenage.

Annabel Wigram at Shephalbury, *c.* 1907.

Family portrait outside the North Star public house in the High Street, *c.* 1898. The photograph was taken by Harry Wilton, a professional photographer with premises in Albert Street.

Ashworth family, *c.* 1920, pictured outside their restaurant at No. 4 Bowling Green. Back row, third from left: Robert Ashworth. Back row, fourth from left: Marion Edith Ashworth. Front row, kneeling: Marnie Ashworth.

Harry MacDonald, the woodcarver of Woolmer Green, *c.* 1954. Harry MacDonald came to Woolmer Green from Yorkshire in 1937. His carved figures began as an advertisement to attract people into his joiner's shop but became a full time occupation.

Harry MacDonald's cottage and garden, *c.* 1954. Visitors came from far and wide to see the sixteenth-century village with its ducking stool and stocks, nursery rhyme characters and castle. After Harry MacDonald's death in 1971 the model village and cottage were both demolished.

SECTION FIVE
Just the Job

Ayres the grocers, *c.* 1890. Ayres was at the south end of the High Street on Trinity Corner. It was proud of its reputation for quality and for its range of goods.

Ayres delivery van outside the store, *c.* 1897. The firm's most exclusive product was their 'Ideal' tea, specially selected and blended to suit the water of the district. At around this time it cost between 1s. 6d. and 2s. 6d. per pound.

Our Mutual Friend public house, No. 52 London Road, said to have been given its name by Charles Dickens. Dickens and Lord Lytton were active in promoting the Guild of Literature and Art in Stevenage and had homes built across the road from the pub for authors and artists who had fallen on hard times. The pub stood on the site of the leisure centre, and after the licence was transferred to a pub in the New Town it became the British Rail Staff and Social Club. Bill Upton was the last licensee.

The North Star, No. 12 High Street, *c.* 1903. The North Star faced the Upper Pond, one of the three ponds at the northern part of the High Street. Jessie Gardner was the licensee for many years until the pub closed down just after the First World War, and she moved to the Dun Cow at Letchmore Green.

Underwood's Saddlers, *c.* 1890. Mr Underwood (left) is standing with his family in front of his shop at No. 58 High Street on the corner of Bridge Road. There were several saddlers in Stevenage at the turn of the century, who made riding equipment and harnesses for farms and for the vehicles that used the Great North Road.

Booker & Co. Cycles, No. 115–17 High Street, *c.* 1905.

Educational Supply Association (ESA), *c.* 1895. The ESA was founded in 1974 by Fennet Appleton and James Pennel Collins. They had started out together in 1868 printing and supplying stationery to schools but soon diversified into school furniture. Their original business was in London but Collins, who lived in Stevenage, bought the iron founders in the town which developed into the Stevenage ESA site.

ESA workers, *c.* 1910, shown outside one of the factory buildings in Fairview Road.

ESA joiners shop, *c.* 1912. The workman in the centre of the picture is building an art desk.

ESA factory interior, *c.* 1942. During the Second World War women were drafted to work alongside men in the factories. Women and men are pictured here making the wings for Mosquito aircraft.

ESA staff, 1949, posed outside the No. 1 Machine Shop in Fairview Road. Back row, left to right: E. Turner, ? Thuragood, J. Henley, W. Saunders, T. Clark, K. Toll, T. Roberts, A. King. Third row, left to right: F. Saunders, D. Wittering, K. Toll, P. Wilkinson, J. Nye, C. Peacock, F. Fairy, J. Swain, H. Hare. Second row, left to right: J. Allen, A. Ansell, L. Smith, F. Davies, F. Hilliar, A. Saunders. E. Cain. Front row, left to right: W. Fox, L. Buckle, W. Cherry, T. Baker, J. Totman, B. Street, W. Swain, ? Jackman, G. Bentley.

O'Clee's delivery cart, *c.* 1903. Mr F.E. O'Clee established the family butchering business at No. 33 High Street in the early 1890s, and opened another shop in Knebworth a few years later.

Harry O'Clee, *c.* 1930.

George and Albert Shelford outside the Record Bakery, *c.* 1915. Shelford's was established around 1800. They made bread and supplied cereals as horse, cattle, poultry and game food. They made ordinary bread and special breads such as 'Turog', 'Silig' and 'No. 1 Farmhouse Bread', which was marketed as being white but possessing nutritious properties not usually found in white bread. The third generation of the family began to sell the bread nationally.

Thomas Phipps, milkman, outside the Chequers public house, *c.* 1913. He is delivering milk from Mr Pallett's Town Dairy. This was at No. 17 High Street, where Mr Pallett kept about twenty cows.

Shepherd's Butchers, No. 65 High Street, *c.* 1920.

Stebbing Farm delivery cart, *c*. 1920. Stebbing Farm was one of the oldest buildings in Fishers Green. The farm, the Fisherman public house and some cottages were the only buildings there in the nineteenth century.

Stebbing's dairy van, *c*. 1930.

Potato picking on Almond Hill, *c.* 1920. The women are wearing hessian sacks as protective clothing over their dresses. From left to right: Mrs Mabel Rawlinson, Mrs Moyes, -?-, 'Mopper' Moyes (the horseman at Fairlands Farm).

Farm cart, *c.* 1928. The cart belonged to John William Smith, whose name appears on the side.

Buckingham's Hairdressers, No. 102 High Street, *c.* 1925. Mr Buckingham, who owned the shop, is standing at the left hand side of the picture.

Horse and cart in Stevenage High Street, *c.* 1930.

Stevenage Urban District Council dustcart outside No. 17 High Street, *c.* 1930. The Urban District Council replaced the Local Board in 1894, its responsibilities including the organization of the fire brigade, water supply and drainage, and public spaces. Refuse collection began in Stevenage in 1906.

C.F. Allen's milk float at Allen's Meadow, Letchmore Road, *c.* 1925, just one of the milk floats made by the Shepherd family business in Back Lane (see page 90).

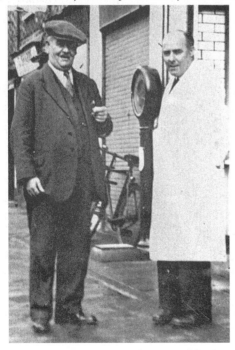

Furr's fish shop, 1950. Mr Furr is standing to the right of Mr Austin outside Furr's at No. 97 High Street.

Vincent HRD motorcycles, *c.* 1950. The road test 1948 series 'B' Rapides are about to be dispatched. From left to right: Joe Harmer, Ted Davis, Alf Searle, -?-.

Vincent three-wheeler car, *c.* 1950. Ted Davis is the driver and Bruce Main-Smith the passenger.

Old town Saturday market, May 1953.

Stevenage market at the Forum, *c.* 1960. The market moved from Market Place in the Old Town to its open-air site at the Forum.

Stevenage market, the Forum, 30 November 1973. The market was situated at the Forum while its eventual home beneath the multi-storey car park was being built. The market moved to its current premises in Market Place a month after this photograph was taken.

New Stevenage market, 7 December 1973.

Kodak canteen, *c.* 1960. Kodak moved into its Development Corporation factory unit in 1954 and employed over 1,500 workers

The Marquis of Lorne, No. 132 High Street, *c.* 1958.

SECTION SIX

Events

The White Lion hotel, No. 60 High Street, decorated in celebration of Queen Victoria's Diamond Jubilee. The White Lion is over 300 years old and some of the original timbers can still be seen inside.

Laying the foundation stone of the Methodist church, 27 July 1876.

Proclamation of King George V, 14 May 1910. A crowd is gathered on the Bowling Green to hear the new king proclaimed, and a platform has been erected for local dignitaries. The local militia, firemen and police are arranged in regimental lines in front of the platform. In the background on the left are Nos 2 and 4 High Street, and on the right are the Bowling Green cottages and the 'Old Cottage'.

Pound Farm in Letchmore Road decorated for George V's coronation celebrations in 1910.

The unveiling of Stevenage War Memorial, March 1921. The memorial was erected in remembrance of those who died in the First World War when the population of the town was only 5,000. More names were added after the Second World War.

Stevenage War Memorial, c. 1921. The memorial is surrounded by wreaths and the building that would become the Publix Cinema can be seen in the background.

Stevenage Hospital Saturday Fund carnival, 1922. The St Nicholas School float in this year was entitled The League of Nations. Mrs Glazebrook is the girl in the fez representing Persia.

Knebworth railway station, 1926. The Reverend Davies (right) is carrying out routine maintenance work with two other men during the General Strike of 1926.

Hospital Saturday Fund carnival float, *c.* 1930. Front row, left: Mr Rowbottoms. Standing in front of the horse: Frederick Bryant. Extreme right, by horse's head: Mr Briars. Mr Briars and Mr Bryant were coalmen in Stevenage who worked for Mr Pearman, a coal-merchant.

Hitchin Hospital carnival float at the Six Hills Nursery, London Road, *c.* 1930. The wheels of the truck were whitened by Ted Bracey and 2,000 Canterbury Bell flowers were used to decorate the float. From left to right: Alfred Wooton, Wilby Nye, Ted Bracey and 'Weeny' Carpenter.

Street party in Walkern Road to celebrate Victory in Europe, 1945.

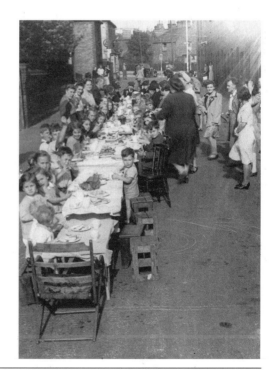

Victory party, Albert Street, 1945. Those present include the Blackwell children, Marie Beedon, Pat Smeaton, Philip Beedon, Doris Carter, Mr and Mrs Mardlin, Mr and Mrs Wittering and Mrs Jackson.

Stevenage Town Football Club anniversary dinner, 1947. The dinner was held in the ESA factory canteen. Left hand table, left side, front to back: Mrs Conlin, Mr Conlin, -?-, -?-, Billie Westwood, Jack Deamer, Vic Folbigg. Left table, right side, front to back: Ken Watson, Mrs Watson, Mr Walsons, Mr Walsons, -?-, -?-, Sammie Lane, -?-. Second table from left, left side, front to back: Lionel Phillips, Nye Wilby, Ronnie Moss, -?-, Ray Palmer, -?-, -?-, Mr Garod, Mr Vicker, -?-, -?-, -?-, -?-, -?-, -?-, -?-, -?-. Second table from left, right side, from front: Mrs Phillips, Vie Bygraves, Reg Luxon, Dutchie Fairey. Second table from right, left side, sixth from front: Mr Peacock. Tenth from front: Les Dye. Eleventh from front: Alfie Stokes. Second table from right, right side, front to back: Mr and Mrs Marvel, Mr and Mrs Scott, -?-, -?-, Harry Dashwood, Mrs Dashwood, -?-, -?-, -?-, -?-, -?-, -?-, -?-, -?-. Standing at the back, left to right: Harry Morris, Mrs Morris, -?-, Percy Wilds, Eddie Henderson, Mrs Henderson, Mr and Mrs Scanlon.

The Twin Foxes public house on its opening day in May 1953. The pub is on Rockingham Way, a piece of land which was once part of the poaching twins' hunting ground.

The Queen Mother visiting a house in the Bedwell area of Stevenage in July 1956.

A party in Stanmore Road church hall, *c*. 1960.

The Queen Mother inspecting guides at St Andrew's church, Abbots Grove, July 1956.

English Electric Company welcoming the Queen, 1959. English Electric later joined with other companies including another New Town industry, De Havilland, to become the British Aircraft Corporation (BAC). In 1977 BAC was nationalized and its name was changed to British Aerospace.

The Prime Minister Harold MacMillan visiting Stevenage, 6 August 1959. He had lunch at Aston House, the headquarters of Stevenage Development Corporation, before moving on to visit the New Town of Harlow

The Queen Mother at the consecration of St George's church on 27 November 1960. A congregation of more than a thousand people witnessed the consecration of the new parish church by the Bishop of St Albans, the Rt. Revd E.M. Gresford. The church was renamed St Andrew and St George's in 1984.

The Prime Minister Harold Wilson visiting the New Town on its twenty-first birthday in 1967. Front row, left to right: Dame Evelyn Denington (Chairwoman, Stevenage Development Corporation), Harold Wilson, George Balderstone (Chairman, Stevenage Urban District Council). Behind them (partly obscured): Bill Lawrence, Philip Ireton, E.J. Bowers. We do not know the name of the child who stole the show!

Releasing balloons outside Stevenage Leisure Centre to celebrate the New Town's fortieth birthday, November 1986. The Rt Hon. John Silkin MP (the son of Lewis Silkin who was Minister of Town and Country Planning in 1946) is standing between the Mayoress, Dora Munden and the Mayor, Stan Munden.

One day stoppage meeting, May 1968. The BAC, G.W. King and ICT factories all stopped work as members of the engineering unions took part in a one day token strike. Smaller factories in the town were also affected.

Mass meeting at the Marks and Spencer building site, 7 May 1969. Two hundred building workers met to show support for five sacked labourers.

GPO engineering strikers, 1969.

Farmers' protest, January 1970. Farmers drove their tractors from Walkern and through Stevenage to St Albans for a protest rally against reduction in their profit margins. Around a hundred farmers from all over Hertfordshire joined in the protest.

Teachers' meeting, 1970. Nine Stevenage schools were affected by a ten day teachers' strike to support their pay claim. Ninety-seven per cent of the Stevenage and District Teachers Association had decided in favour of strike action.

Mortgage marchers, 1975. More than 500 Stevenage Borough Council mortgagors voted at a packed public meeting on Tuesday 11 March to withhold their payments in protest against the Council's decision to raise the rate from 12 to 14½ per cent. They followed this with a demonstration in London to the Prices Minister and to Shirley Williams, Stevenage's MP.

SECTION SEVEN

At Your Service

Stevenage Fire Brigade, 1897, standing outside Orchard Court in Orchard Road – decorated to celebrate Queen Victoria's Diamond Jubilee.

Stevenage Fire Brigade outside No. 38 High Street, 1953, when they brought out their old horse-drawn fire engine and uniforms for the coronation celebrations of Elizabeth II.

Fire Brigade at ESA fire in Fairview Road, 1907.

ESA factory fire, Fairview Road, 1907. Part of the fire engine used to fight the fire stands in front of the burnt out building.

Stevenage Fire Brigade, *c.* 1937. Two fire engines outside the station in Basils Road.

National Fire Service firemen with an Austin towing vehicle, during the Second World War. Left to right: Halling, Palmer, Pratt, Rolph, Lintott, Hunt.

ESA Fire Brigade during the Second World War, behind a fire engine with a trophy that they have won.

Stevenage Fire Station, Basils Road, during the Second World War. Far left: Joe Shepherd.

Gas House, No. 2 Letchmore Road, *c.* 1897. Built in the sixteenth century, the house served as the parish workhouse from 1773 until 1835. In 1855 it became the offices of the Stevenage Gas, Light and Coke Company. The gasworks was beside the house.

Stevenage First World War nursing group, *c.* 1915. The dress of some of the women suggests that they are putting on a play.

The old post office, No. 52 High Street, *c.* 1900. It was the first post office in Stevenage and was built in 1887. Next door to it at the far left of the picture is Fressons chemist shop.

The new post office, No. 13 High Street, soon after construction. The post office moved here in 1909 from No. 52. There was a large sorting room at the back.

The Stevenage platoon in Reading, 1914.

Red Cross nurses, *c.* 1925.

Stevenage Ambulance Corps, *c.* 1939. This was set up in 1929.

Invasion exercise, Trinity church, 28 June 1942.

Stevenage Home Guard at Alleynes School, *c.* 1943. The official title was 26 Platoon, C Company, 2nd Battalion, Hertfordshire Home Guard. Middle row, far left: Ernie Pumfrey. Fourth from left: Mr Inglefield. Second from right: Mr Wittering. Front row, from left to right: Mr Aldridge, -?-, -?-, Mr Toll (Sergeant), Mr Bulleid (Lieutenant), Mr Allen, Mr Saville, -?-, -?-.

Home Guard parade at the presentation of an armoured car, Walkern Road/High Street, 28 July 1940. The car was converted by Mr Appleton of the ESA by adding steel plates to the chassis. It was designed to carry three machine guns and a crew of five.

Home Guard inspection, Walkern Road, 28 July 1940. Mrs Appleton and Major-General Tindal-Lucas are inspecting the guard of honour.

Women's Voluntary Service cart, *c.* 1940. The Women's Voluntary Service was founded in 1938 to help the war effort. It ran rest centres and canteens, organized emergency transport and escorted evacuees.

Women's Voluntary Service canteen staff, *c.* 1945. The Stevenage WVS ran the Old Castle Canteen in Middle Row. The staff are pictured here with the British and American military badges they collected from visiting servicemen.

Hertfordshire Home Guard, 2C Company in 1945. They are parading in the High Street to celebrate VE Day.

Red Cross nurses, during the Second World War.

Gas Air Raid Patrol, 1941, outside the Urban District Council Gas Depot in Church Lane. The four men in the front row with the two stirrup pumps are civilians employed by the Gas Board to turn off the gas in the event of burst pipes before the rescue team moved in. The men in the back row are Home Guard members in uniform.

Stevenage air raid patrol, c. 1940. The men are standing outside the Fisherman public house in Fishers Green.

Group of Territorial soldiers from the Hertfordshire Regiment during the First World War.

Stevenage Fire Brigade in the VE Day parade, 1945, passing the Cromwell Hotel in the High Street. In the centre of the front row of three firemen is Mr H.G. Lintott.

Stevenage Boy Scouts' parade, High Street, *c.* 1950.

Hertfordshire County Council mobile baby clinic, 1960. In the early days of the New Town, before all services were in place, residents relied on mobile services for many of their needs.

Freedom from Hunger campaign,
town centre, 5 April 1963.

Stevenage Round Table Red Cross, 15 May 1964. Fourth from right: Winifred Boyd.

Ambulance workers' strike, 1969. The five Stevenage ambulance women and fourteen men voted unanimously to support the London members of the Federation of Ambulance Personnel, who were calling for recognition of their Union. Emergency calls were answered as usual while routine calls were covered by the Hitchin and Letchworth stations.

Sea cadets forming a Guard of Honour at the Remembrance Day service in 1972.

Schooldays

A group of teachers at St Nicholas School House, North Road, *c.* 1890. The school was opened on 1 January 1834 and was attended by 91 girls and 116 boys. The school closed in July 1963 and reopened in new premises in Six Hills Way.

Class Four at St Nicholas School, *c.* 1900.

Langley School, 1910. Miss Fells was the headmistress at this time.

Miss Beaver's school, 1912. The children are pictured after performing their school play in the school garden.

St Nicholas School girls' class, 1913. Back row, second from right: Glad Grey. Far right: Lillian Ellis. Third row, fifth from right: Aldous. Far right: G. Fox. Second row, left to right: W. Farr, Agnes Allen, Winnie Bryant, -?-, -?-, L. Austin, Gladys Carpenter, -?-, -?-, -?-. Front row, left to right: Hemmings, G. Taplin, Nelly Day, Gladys Troy, -?-, Ivy Tooley, L. Newberry, -?-, Rose Olieph, -?-, Nelly Kirby.

Shephall School on Shephall Green, 1913. Maggie Colliver, aged eight, (now Mrs Deards) is on the second row from the front, second from the left.

Letchmore Road School gardening class, *c.* 1923.

Westover School, *c.* 1923. Westover was a private school taking pupils from Stevenage, Gravely, Digswell, Walkern, Redcoats and Chells. Back row, left to right: Ruth Bull, Barbara Chittuck, Valerie Catling, Joan Cherry, Nancy Wilkinson, Nancy Driver, Nancy Corfield. Third row, left to right: Barbara Carling, Joe Elliott, Mary Hunter, Doris Middlemist, Nancy Bull, Sarah Turnbull, Pamela Patterson, Bill Mason, Barbara Wright, Sylvia Heath, Irene Pike, Edie Keysell, -?-, Bobby Butterfield, -?-. Second row, left to right: Molly Parker, -?-, Hazel Popple, -?-, -?-, -?-, Trevor Wilkinson, Mary Oddie, -?-, Dick Butterfield, David Cherry. Front row, left to right: Michael Apted, Guy Hunter, -?-, Marjorie Thorne, -?-, -?-, John Apted.

Stevenage Grammar School cricket team, *c*. 1920.

Alleynes School football team, 1928/9. Back row, left to right: E.H. Watson, R.G. Bowles, K.S. Hammond. Middle row, left to right: K.G. Prater, A.W. Drury, S.G. Bunting (Captain), W.V. Franklin, S.H. Sheppard. Front row, left to right: J.S. Mackay, G.F. Franklin, J. Savill.

Girls' class at St Nicholas School, 1924/5.

Shephall School, Shephall Green, *c.* 1930. Front row, third from right: Miss M. Spicer.

Alleynes School play, 1946. From 1945 the Christmas drama production was an annual feature of school life. The play in 1946 was Shakespeare's *Twelfth Night*.

Alleynes Christmas production, 1949. The cast poses after its performance of Shakespeare's *The Taming of the Shrew*.

Alleynes School hockey team, 1953.

Alleynes School teachers, 1958. They are walking through the school yard on their way to the dedication of the school organ on the school's 400th anniversary.

Sports day at Alleynes School, 1960.

Mossbury Primary School, *c.* 1960.

Pear Tree Junior School, 1964. The children are standing by a model of the town centre which they made during the summer term.

Bandley Hill School, 16 October 1964. The children are taking part in harvest festival celebrations, and are dressed in the national costumes of different countries.

Peartree Spring Junior School football team, 26 March 1964. The team are being presented with the Stevenage Primary Schools' FA Cup by Wally Barnes.

Longmeadow Athletic football club, c. 1965. The team is at the front of the group with the supporters behind.

Acknowledgements

All of the photographs in this book have been loaned or donated to Stevenage Museum and massive thanks are due to everyone who has contributed to Stevenage Museum's collection over the years. Thanks are also due to Gwynneth Grimwood, Anthony and Peter Nicolson, Paula Campbell and Hugh Madgin.

Picture Credits

Mr B.G. Ashman: pp. 42 (top), 112 (bottom). Bedford Lemere & Co.: p. 99 (bottom). Mr E.V. Lock: pp. 36 (top), 111 (top and bottom). Mr G.L. Blake: pp. 28 (top and bottom), 33, 43 (top and bottom), 44, 47 (top and bottom), 65 (bottom), 80 (top), 110 (top), 112 (top), 121 (top), 144 (bottom). Intercity: p. 53 (top). *Comet and Gazette*: pp. 24 (bottom), 25 (bottom), 26, 31 (top and bottom), 48 (bottom), 53 (bottom), 54, 66 (top and bottom), 67, 122 (top and bottom), 125 (top and bottom), 137 (bottom), 145 (bottom), 158 (bottom), 159 (top). Francis Frith Collection: p. 41 (bottom). Mr P. James: p. 36 (bottom). Mr E.W. Kingsland: p. 146 (bottom). Keystone Press Agency Ltd: p. 64. Mr P. Newman: p. 22. J. Sainsbury plc: p. 30 (top). Leslie Slipsides Ltd: p. 45 (top). Studio Libra: pp. 27 (bottom), 29 (top and bottom), 80 (bottom), 157 (bottom), 158 (top).